AR Quiz
1.0 pts
MG 6.6

Beach Park Middle School LRC
40667 N. Green Bay Road
Beach Park, IL 60099

INCREDIBLE TRUE ADVENTURES
THE CURSE OF KING TUT'S TOMB
AND OTHER ANCIENT DISCOVERIES

ANITA GANERI & DAVID WEST

rosen publishing's
rosen central
New York

Published in 2012 by The Rosen Publishing Group, Inc.
29 East 21st Street, New York, NY 10010

Designed and produced by
David West Books

Copyright © 2012 David West Books

All rights reserved. No part of this book may be reproduced in any form without permission in writing from the publisher, except by a reviewer.

Designer: Gary Jeffrey
Editor: Katharine Pethick
Illustrator: David West

Picture credits:

4–5, nikoreto; 5t, Xerones; 8bl Gérard Ducher; 9bl, Kaveh; 11m, Jiashiang Wang; 12b, 13b, Bernt Rostad; 12mr, Georges Jansoone; 13tr, Tomasz Sienicki; 13tl, inyucho; 17tmr, Britrob; 16–17, Ming-yen Hsu; 24b, Library of Congress, Prints and Photographs Division; 24br, Pirate Alice; 25tl, Paul Stevenson; 25mr, Claus Ableiter; 25br, Patricio Lorente; 25m, Beatrix; 29br, Tom Tarrant; 32mb, Marie-Lan Nguyen; 32br, Marshall Astor; p32tr, peuplier; 33mtr, Steve Swayne; 33mr, Andree Stephan; 32–33m, Armin; 33br, Wolfgang Sauber; p37ml, Bjørn Giesenbauer; 40–41main, Menage a Moi; 41t, WordRidden; 41mr, wit; 41mbr, IH (40); 41br, Dr Steven Plunkett; 41bl, Nancy Waterfall; 41tl, minophis; 40m, Shannon Hobbs; 45br, soyignatius; 45tr, Alex Steffler; 45mbr, José Porras;

Library of Congress Cataloging-in-Publication Data

Ganeri, Anita, 1961-
 The curse of King Tut's tomb and other ancient discoveries / Anita Ganeri, David West.
   p. cm. -- (Incredible true adventures)
 Includes bibliographical references and index.
 ISBN 978-1-4488-6657-1 (library binding) -- ISBN 978-1-4488-6661-8 (pbk.) -- ISBN 978-1-4488-6669-4 (6-pack)
 1. Archaeology--Juvenile literature. 2. Antiquities--Juvenile literature. 3. Civilization, Ancient--Juvenile literature. I. West, David. II. Title.
 CC171.G36 2012
 930.1--dc23
                                                          2011031167

Printed in China

CPSIA Compliance Information Batch #DWW12YA:
For further information contact Rosen Publishing, New York, New York, at 1-800-237-9932.

CONTENTS

INTRODUCTION	4
THE CURSE OF TUTANKHAMUN	6
Raiding the Dead	8
THE TERRACOTTA ARMY	10
Soldiers of Qin	12
THE LEGEND OF TROY	14
Layers of Truth	16
THE BODY IN THE ICE	18
Examining Ötzi	20
POMPEII	22
City of Ashes	24
SWARTKRANS CAVEBOY	26
CSI Swartkrans	28
IN THE PALACE OF MINOS	30
Into the Labyrinth?	32
THE DEATH OF PETE MARSH	34
Ritual Murder	36
BURIAL AT SUTTON HOO	38
Whose Grave?	40
THE LOST CITY OF COPÁN	42
Clues to the Past	44
GLOSSARY & FURTHER INFORMATION	46
INDEX	48

INTRODUCTION

Egyptian mummies hidden for centuries. Fabulous tombs and treasures lost from sight. Ancient bodies buried in mysterious circumstances. When these ancient discoveries were found, often by accident, they caused great excitement and provided a glimpse into history. Their stories make fascinating reading, as they offer up their secrets from the past.

An archaeological dig unearths more of ancient Rome.

An amazingly well preserved Egyptian mummy in a museum

FIND OUT MORE

THE CURSE OF TUTANKHAMUN
"I can see things, *wonderful* things!"

As he spoke, Howard Carter felt a wave of relief that Tutankhamun's tomb hadn't been robbed bare. Beside him, his backer, Lord Carnarvon, stood grinning—after years of searching, his investment might finally pay off. It was November 24, 1922, and the moment of truth had arrived at last.

Three weeks earlier, after a seven-year search, Carter had found a staircase leading to a sealed door bearing the name of the boy-king. Beyond that, a rubble-filled passageway led to another door. Chipping a small hole in the door, Carter held up a candle and peered into the chamber beyond. What he saw took his breath away. The room was filled with priceless treasure—chariots, couches, statues—sparkling with gold and hidden from human eyes for more than 3,000 years. Surely this must be the antechamber to the pharaoh's tomb?

Over the next few months, Carter painstakingly catalogued and removed each item from the antechamber. Then, he turned his attention to a sealed doorway in one of the walls. Carefully, Carter chipped away at the plaster to reveal… a huge, wooden shrine, covered in gold. In the center of the shrine were two doors that opened to three smaller shrines, but the most exciting find was yet to come. At the center of the main shrine was a stone sarcophagus, and inside a solid gold coffin lay the body of Tutankhamun himself!

As with many of the ancient shrines that had warnings written around them, it was said that anyone who disturbed a dead pharaoh would be cursed. Over the years, several people connected with the discovery of Tutankhamun's tomb died in mysterious ways. Was the pharaoh's curse true, after all?

FIND OUT MORE

RAIDING THE DEAD

One person who dismissed the idea of a curse was Howard Carter himself. He died in 1939, at the age of 64, of natural causes. Many others who visited the tomb lived long and healthy lives.

Carter examining the contents of the sarcophagus

Tomb Treasures

In ancient Egypt, the dead were buried with everything they needed for the afterlife. Some 2,000 priceless objects were found in Tutankhamun's tomb, including his exquisite death mask.

A golden throne (below) is decorated with portraits of Tutankhamun and his wife.

Carved head of Tutankhamun emerging from a lotus flower

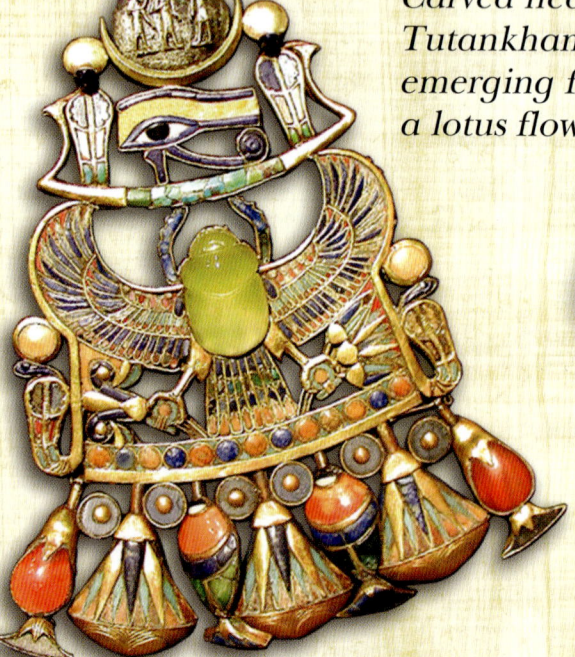

This beautiful pendant is made from gold, silver, and semi-precious stones.

A solar scarab pendant

8

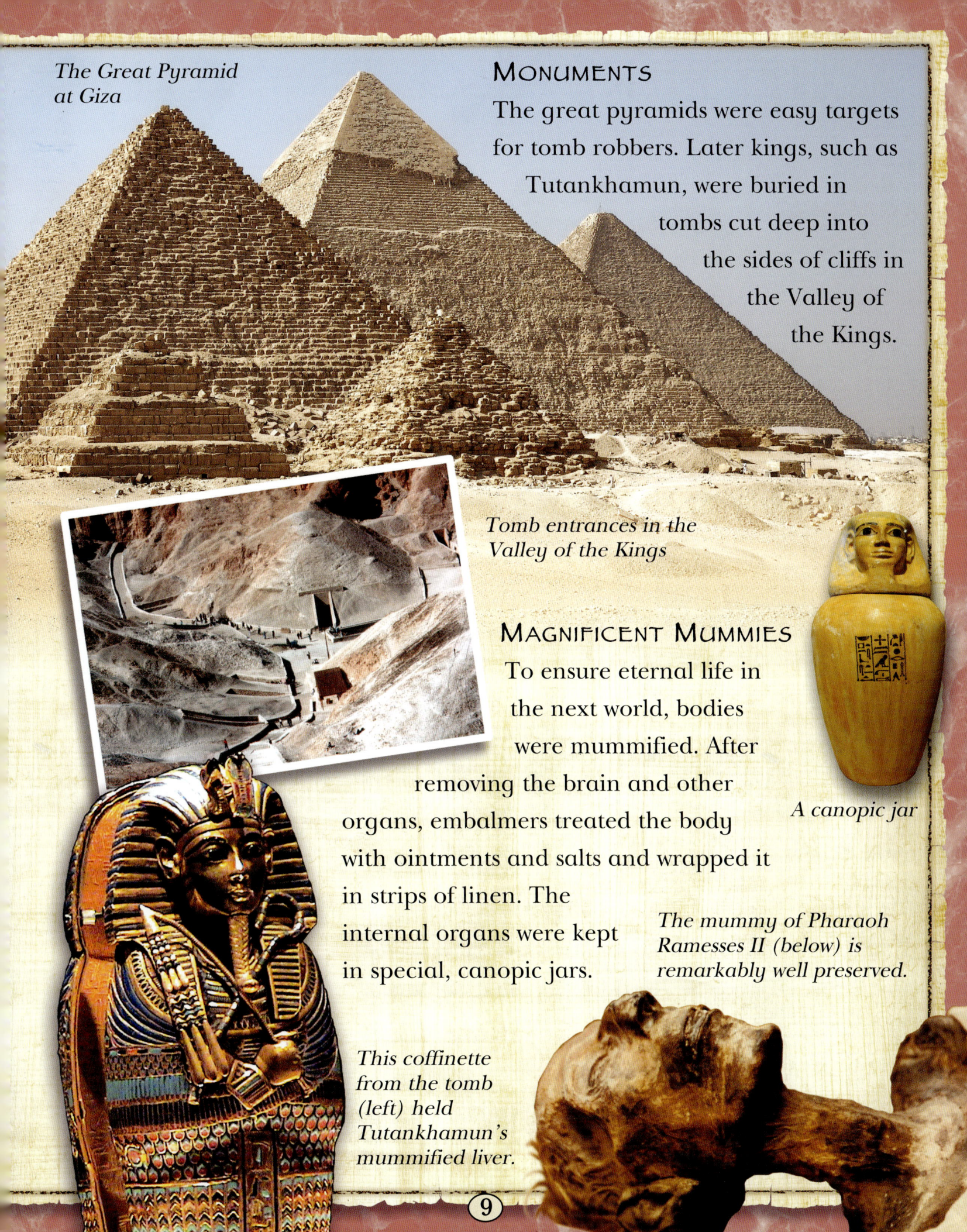

The Great Pyramid at Giza

MONUMENTS

The great pyramids were easy targets for tomb robbers. Later kings, such as Tutankhamun, were buried in tombs cut deep into the sides of cliffs in the Valley of the Kings.

Tomb entrances in the Valley of the Kings

MAGNIFICENT MUMMIES

To ensure eternal life in the next world, bodies were mummified. After removing the brain and other organs, embalmers treated the body with ointments and salts and wrapped it in strips of linen. The internal organs were kept in special, canopic jars.

A canopic jar

The mummy of Pharaoh Ramesses II (below) is remarkably well preserved.

This coffinette from the tomb (left) held Tutankhamun's mummified liver.

As he shouted out in surprise, the man turned the object over with his spade. He had expected to find a simple lump of earth, but instead he found himself staring at a remarkably life-like human head made from clay. It was extremely detailed and like nothing he had ever seen before. Calling his friends over, the farmer put the head carefully to one side and carried on digging.

The men were local farmers from Xiyang Village, in Shaanxi Province, central China. It was 1974, and, following a long, dry winter, the water supplies in the region were running low. The crops needed watering, so the men were digging a well one-and-a-half miles (2.4 km) east of nearby Mount Lishan.

As they dug further, they discovered part of a beautifully made, clay body that looked like a soldier, buried in a pit, together with some pieces of rusty metal. But who did these mysterious objects belong to and what were they going to do with them?

Unbeknownst to the farmers, they had stumbled upon one of the most amazing archaeological finds of the 20th century, now regarded as the eighth wonder of the ancient world. The head belonged to a life-like and life-sized terracotta (clay) soldier, part of a huge, buried army.

For 2,000 years, this Terracotta Army had guarded the tomb of Qin (pronounced "Chin") Shi Huangdi, the first emperor of China. The soldiers were laid out in military formation, ready to fight for their ruler. The tomb was said to look like an underground city, with a throne room, a treasury, watchtowers, walls, and gates, and rivers made of mercury.

The farmers decided to take their discoveries to the authorities. A few weeks later, a team of archaeologists arrived in the village and began to excavate the site. As they dug, they uncovered more figures, but how many more were to come?

FIND OUT MORE

SOLDIERS OF QIN

To date, more than 8,000 soldiers and horses have been recovered. The soldiers had once held real bronze weapons, ready to defend the tomb from attack, alongside charioteers with full-sized chariots.

ETERNAL EMPEROR

Soon after becoming emperor, Qin Shi Huangdi began preparations for his tomb. It took 700,000 workmen some 36 years to build. To keep him safe in the afterlife, Qin also ordered the Terracotta Army to be created.

Most of the figures were broken and had to be painstakingly restored.

Traces of color on the figures (left) show that they were once brightly painted (right).

The terracotta warriors are now housed in a specially built museum close to the tomb (below).

A life-sized bronze swan was found beside an underground stream.

There are two large-scale bronze chariots with terracotta figures (left and below).

Terra Treasures

Soon after the emperor's death in 210 BCE, the tomb was raided by rebel soldiers. They set fire to the complex, burying the Terracotta Army in ash and mud. Only one figure survived intact—a kneeling archer (opposite).

A reproduction terracotta statue of Emperor Qin is flanked by two commanders as he surveys his clay army.

THE LEGEND OF TROY
"Behold, a gift from the Greeks!"

The sentry rubbed his eyes in disbelief. For ten long years of war, the Trojans had woken every morning to find the Greek army surrounding their walls. But today, the soldiers were gone and in their place stood a huge wooden horse. Believing it signaled the end of the war, the Trojans dragged the horse into the city and began to celebrate. But was everything as it seemed?

According to Greek mythology, the story of the Trojan War began in Sparta, where Paris, prince of Troy, had gone as an ambassador. There he fell madly in love with Helen, the wife of Menelaus, king of Sparta, and said to be the most beautiful woman in the world. Paris persuaded her to sail back home with him.

Furious, Menelaus vowed revenge. Soon a fleet of a thousand ships, led by Agamemnon, the brother of Menelaus, was carrying the Greek army to Troy.

Troy was rich and powerful, defended by massive stone walls. Unable to force their way in, the Greeks laid siege, with bitter fighting and great losses on both sides. With no end to the siege in sight, the Greek hero, Odysseus, came up with a cunning plan. He would fill a wooden horse with soldiers and send it into Troy.

As the Trojans celebrated, the soldiers climbed out of the horse, opened the city gates... and let the Greek army inside.

The story of the Trojan War was told by the Greek poet, Homer, in his *Iliad*. But was Troy a real city or a myth?

FIND OUT MORE

LAYERS OF TRUTH

By the 19th century, most scholars believed that Troy and the Trojan war had never existed. However, Bunarbashi, in western Turkey, was claimed by a few to be the historical site for the great city.

THE DISCOVERY

In the 1870s, German archaeologist Heinrich Schliemann started excavating at Hissarlik, a small hill a couple of miles (3.2 km) from Bunarbashi. There, he discovered the ruins of a series of ancient cities. Near the bottom was a layer, which Schliemann declared to be Troy.

Schliemann (above right) also made famous finds at other ancient cities, including this gold mask from Mycenae in Greece.

A statue of Homer, author of the Iliad, which told of the Trojan war

Trojan prince Aeneas flees a burning Troy. The city was thoroughly sacked by the triumphant Greeks.

THE JEWELS OF HELEN

Schliemann unearthed a wealth of artifacts at Hissarlik. The most famous was a gold headdress, which he claimed had belonged to Helen herself. It is now known that these treasures date from a much earlier period.

The Schliemann treasure haul

Schliemann's wife wearing the "jewels of Helen"

The actual city (right) appears to have been much smaller than the one of Homeric legend.

Archaeologists have excavated parts of the massive stone walls (above) that surrounded the city of Troy.

At Hissarlik, the digging continues. These silver coins come from the Roman city of Ilium, which lies in the top layer, about a thousand years after the fall of Troy.

THE BODY IN THE ICE
"Helmut, we must contact the police!"

As she called to her husband, Erika Simon looked down at the head and shoulders jutting out of the ice. The Simons were returning from a long hike in the mountains close to the border between Austria and Italy. They were convinced they'd found the body of a missing climber, tragically caught in an avalanche. But were they right?

The body was lying on its front, frozen into the ice from the waist down. In the weeks that followed, the Austrian authorities worked on freeing it from its icy grave. Their rough handling damaged the corpse's clothing and left a hole in his hip, and more mishandling followed. Finally, the ice man was taken to the University of Innsbruck where it was examined by experts. The results were astonishing.

Incredibly, the Simons had not found a modern corpse. Instead, they had stumbled on a 5,000-year-old man whose body had become trapped in the ice after he had been killed.

The scientists quickly realized how important their find was. From now on, the man, nicknamed Ötzi, was stored in a freezer to stop further decay. But many questions remained. Who was this man? How did he die? And how had his body survived so well?

FIND OUT MORE

EXAMINING ÖTZI

From the type of copper axe Ötzi carried, experts believe that he lived around 3300 BCE. Because his body froze very quickly after his death, it remained very well preserved until its discovery in 1991.

5,000-year-old Autopsy

At first, experts thought Ötzi had died of exposure during a winter storm. Later tests showed an arrowhead stuck in one shoulder, cuts and bruises to his body, and evidence of a blow to his head. All of this pointed to a violent death, possibly at the hands of a rival tribe.

Ötzi's body (left) was in generally good condition—even his brain, eyeballs, and some hair were intact.

Perhaps Ötzi was involved in a skirmish with a rival tribe? He may have been attacked by a raiding party (below) on his way to deliver the copper axe.

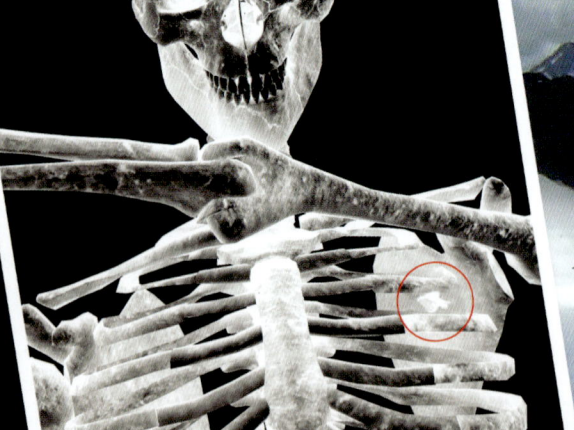

X-rays (left) showed an arrowhead in one of Ötzi's shoulders.

Ötzi's Gear

Many extraordinary objects were found alongside Ötzi's body. These included copper and stone weapons and fungus for lighting a fire. His kit also featured pieces of over a dozen different plants, in addition to flint and pyrite for creating sparks.

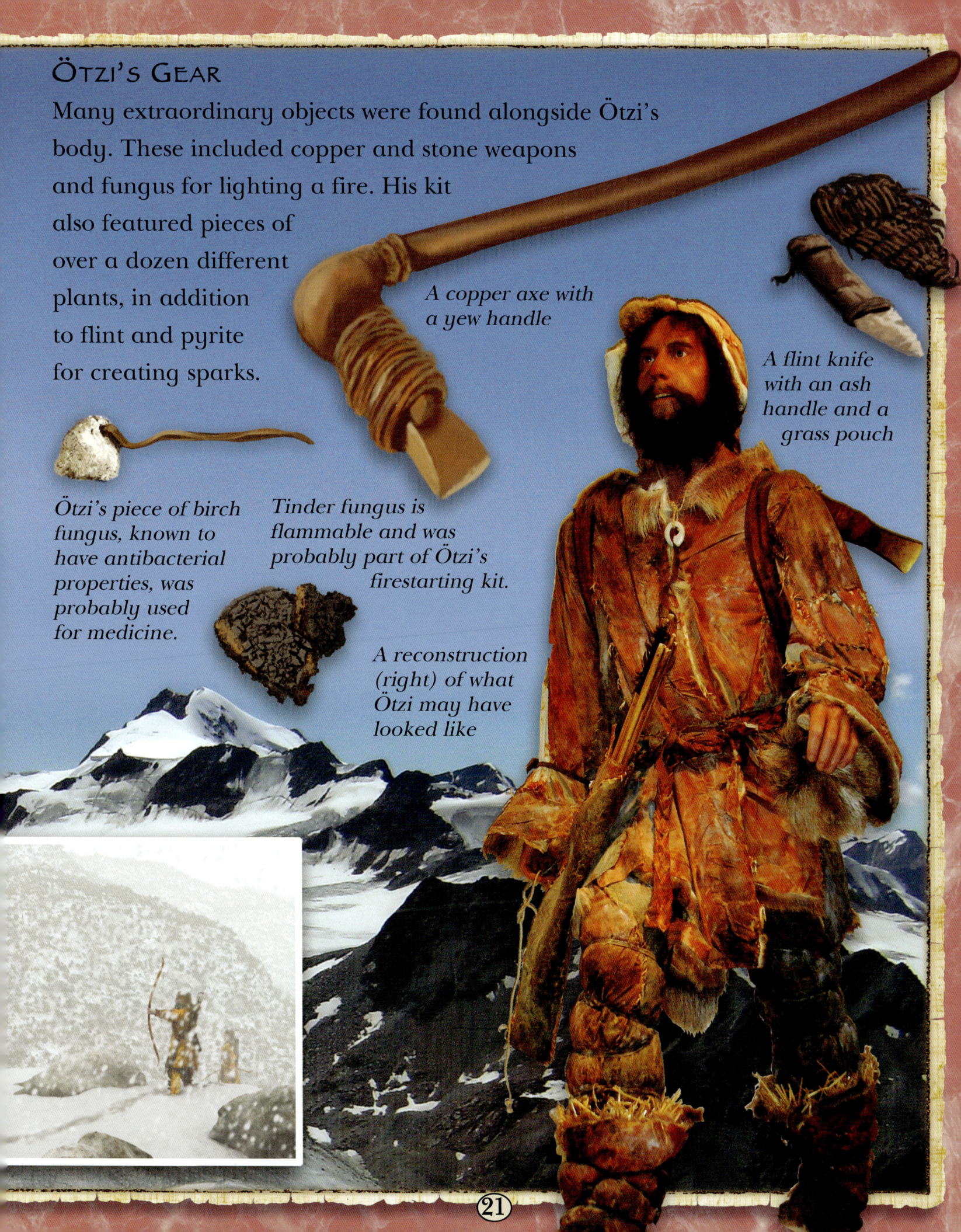

A copper axe with a yew handle

A flint knife with an ash handle and a grass pouch

Ötzi's piece of birch fungus, known to have antibacterial properties, was probably used for medicine.

Tinder fungus is flammable and was probably part of Ötzi's firestarting kit.

A reconstruction (right) of what Ötzi may have looked like

POMPEII
"Father, I can't breathe!"

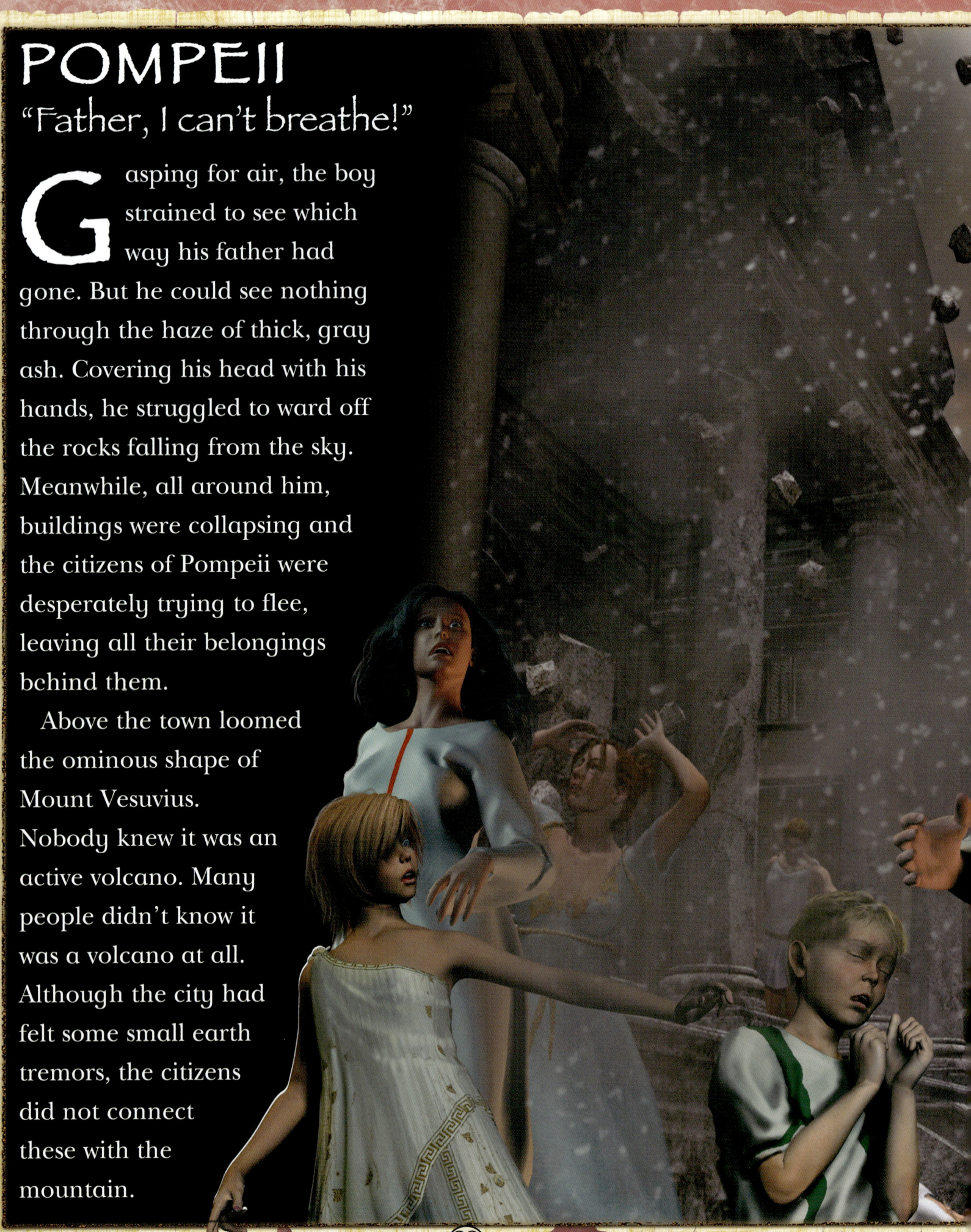

Gasping for air, the boy strained to see which way his father had gone. But he could see nothing through the haze of thick, gray ash. Covering his head with his hands, he struggled to ward off the rocks falling from the sky. Meanwhile, all around him, buildings were collapsing and the citizens of Pompeii were desperately trying to flee, leaving all their belongings behind them.

Above the town loomed the ominous shape of Mount Vesuvius. Nobody knew it was an active volcano. Many people didn't know it was a volcano at all. Although the city had felt some small earth tremors, the citizens did not connect these with the mountain.

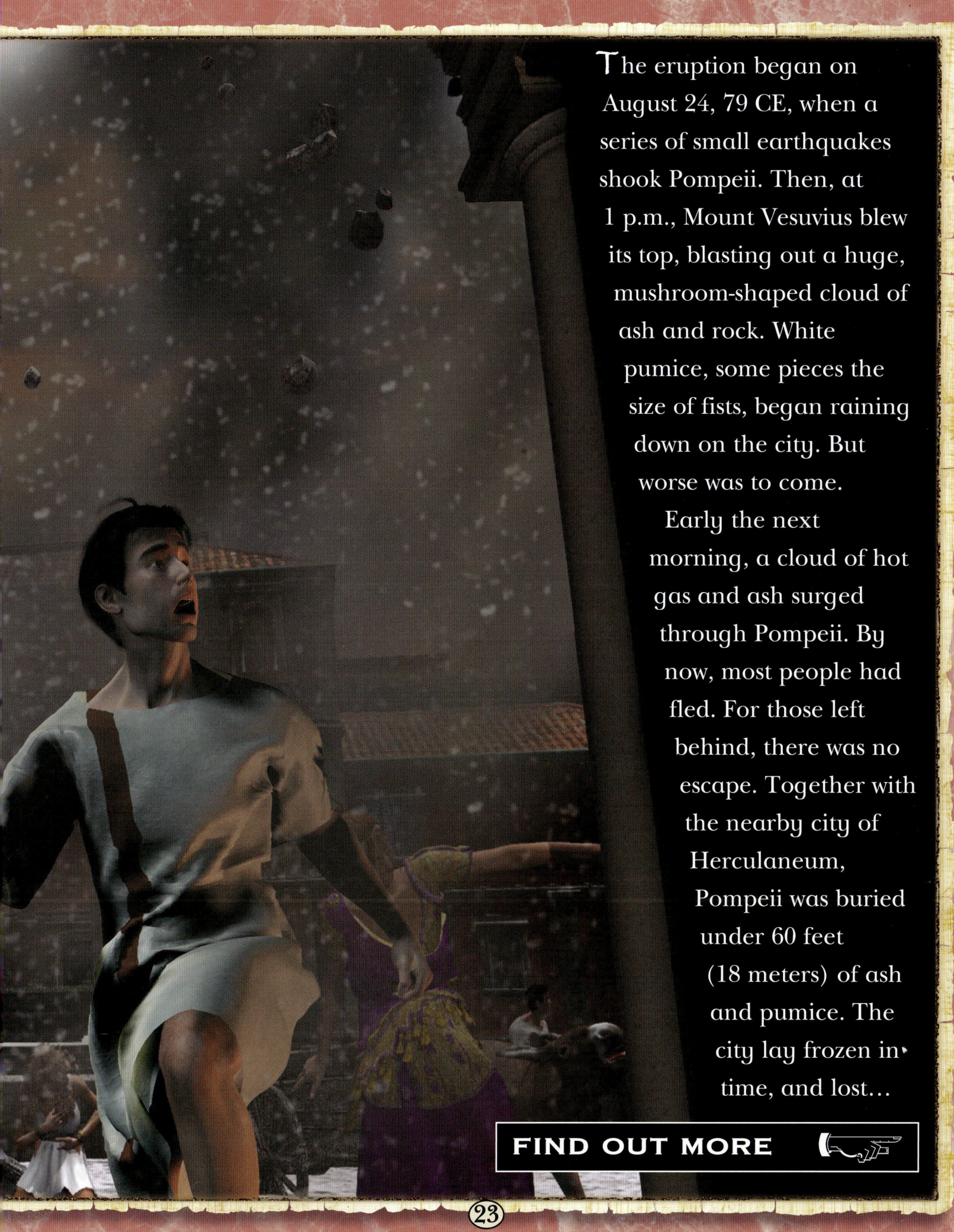

The eruption began on August 24, 79 CE, when a series of small earthquakes shook Pompeii. Then, at 1 p.m., Mount Vesuvius blew its top, blasting out a huge, mushroom-shaped cloud of ash and rock. White pumice, some pieces the size of fists, began raining down on the city. But worse was to come.

Early the next morning, a cloud of hot gas and ash surged through Pompeii. By now, most people had fled. For those left behind, there was no escape. Together with the nearby city of Herculaneum, Pompeii was buried under 60 feet (18 meters) of ash and pumice. The city lay frozen in time, and lost…

FIND OUT MORE

CITY OF ASHES

Blanketed by ash, Pompeii lay forgotten for almost 1,700 years. It was accidentally discovered in 1748 by Spanish engineer Rocque Joaquin de Alcubierre.

Portraits of the city's inhabitants (left and below) from walls in houses in Pompeii

Roman Time Capsule

The layer of ash that buried Pompeii kept it remarkably well preserved, and extensive excavation has led to extraordinary finds. These allow us to travel back in time and glimpse life in a large, thriving city at the height of the Roman Empire.

Ruins of a Thermopolium (above) —the Roman equivalent of a fast food restaurant

A view of Pompeii from 1900 showing the city suburbs

The streets of Pompeii today

ANCIENT MAUSOLEUM

About 2,000 of Pompeii's inhabitants died, suffocated by the hot ash. Over time, the ash set hard around their bodies, while the soft flesh rotted away. By injecting plaster into the spaces left behind, archaeologists have created plaster casts of some of the victims.

Detail from a decorative mosaic

Many amazing buildings, including an amphitheater (left), have been excavated.

Some of the plaster casts of victims (above) can be seen among the ruins of Pompeii.

Artifacts unearthed at Pompeii include glassware (above), statues (right), and even loaves of bread (left).

The forum at Pompeii

Paleontologist and doctor, Professor Robert Broom shook his head in puzzlement as he examined the skull bone in his hand. Even though it was just a fragment, Broom could see it had belonged to a young *Paranthropus robustus*, an early hominid, or apeman. It was the two holes he noticed in the back of the skull that had Broom baffled. With no sign of bone healing, these must have been made either just before or soon after the boy's death.

Inspired by the recent discovery of human-like fossils by the well-known anthropologist Raymond Dart, Broom had begun excavating the limestone cave at Swartkrans in South Africa a year earlier. Among the wealth of early hominid and animal bones he had found, this skull was definitely the most intriguing.

Had the holes been made by a sharp, stone weapon? Had the caveboy been murdered? Had the apemen, in fact, been violent killers? To Broom, this seemed the likeliest explanation.

For a while, the trail went cold. Then, years later, the mystery of the Swartkrans "caveboy" was picked up again by noted South African paleontologist, Professor C.K. "Bob" Brain. As director of the Transvaal Museum, Brain had already built up a strong reputation as an expert in hominid remains.

In 1965, Brain took over the excavations at Swartkrans. For more than 20 years, he examined the hundreds of bones that were found in the cave to try to find out how the animals, and apemen, had lived and died. One day, as he examined the holes in the caveboy's skull, Brain was struck by a sudden and brilliant thought. From his years of research, Brain knew he had seen similar marks somewhere else. At last it came to him, and he believed that he knew how the Swartkran's caveboy had died. His theory was startlingly different from Broom's...

FIND OUT MORE

CSI SWARTKRANS

Brain had seen such marks on the skulls of modern baboons attacked by leopards. In his book, *The Hunters or the Hunted?* he suggested that, far from being killers, the early hominids had actually been preyed on by big cats.

The Sterkfontein caves are the longest continuously running fossil excavations in the world.

Dangerous World

Brain believed that the likeliest predator was a *dinofelis*, the powerfully built, sabre-toothed cat. Fossils show that it preyed on mammoth calves, baboons… and early hominids.

The caveboy's skull with the two bite holes clearly visible

Sabre-tooth cats were the top predators of the Pliocene era.

A dinofelis (below) was about the size of a jaguar, with two large, sharp canine teeth. It may have bitten into the caveboy's skull as it carried its prey into a tree.

This diagram shows what might have happened. Having killed the caveboy, the dinofelis carried the body up into a tree to feed. Eventually, the bones fell out of the tree and were washed into the cave.

THE BONEYARD

Swartkrans Cave is not the only place in South Africa where fossil hominid bones have been found. Other cave sites are Kromdraii and Sterkfontein. Because of these finds, this area has become known as the "Cradle of Humankind."

The skull of a hominid child, found in Taung, South Africa, in 1924. Marks on the skull show that it was probably killed by an eagle.

IN THE PALACE OF MINOS
"Flee, flee—it is the end of us!"

As the terrified Minoans tried to escape, the palace began collapsing around them. Seconds earlier, an earthquake had struck, violently shaking the ground and tearing great cracks in the walls. There had been no warning, and there was nowhere for them to run.

About 30,000 people lived in and around the palace of Knossos on Crete. Here, in his magnificent throne room, the king presided over religious ceremonies and affairs of state. Now, the palace and its throne room lay in ruins, and the king was nowhere to be seen.

But there was worse to come. About 60 miles (100 kilometers) to the north of Crete lay the island of Thera (now known as Santorini). Shortly after the earthquake, around 1500 BCE, the island blew itself apart in one of the most violent eruptions ever known. The blast triggered a deadly tsunami that swept across the ocean, then roared inland, bringing further devastation to the coast of Crete.

Although Knossos was later rebuilt, Minoan culture was seriously weakened and began to decline. It finally collapsed when Crete was invaded by people called the Mycenaeans, from mainland Greece. The Minoans had no power to fight back, and their once glorious civilization seemed doomed to fade into obscurity. But had it been lost for good?

FIND OUT MORE

INTO THE LABYRINTH?

For years, Knossos was only known as the mythical home of the legendary King Minos and the dreaded Minotaur, who lived in the maze-like labyrinth. Then, in 1900, English archaeologist Arthur Evans began to excavate the site.

Part of Arthur Evans's reconstruction of the palace at Knossos

Bull Worship

The bull was sacred in Minoan culture and images of bulls' horns appear all over Knossos. One of the strangest rituals was bull-leaping, where the leaper grasped a bull's horns and jumped on to its back.

A ceremonial drinking cup in the shape of a bull's head

An ivory figurine of a bull leaper discovered at the Knossos site

Arthur Evans

Coins found decorated with mazes and bull-headed men appear to confirm Knossos as the location for the Minotaur's legendary labyrinth.

Theseus slays the Minotaur. The brave Greek king was the legendary founder of Athens.

Palace of Mazes

The palace has 1,300 rooms that are connected with corridors of varying sizes and direction. Some scholars think that it was the palace itself that gave rise to the legend of the labyrinth in Greek mythology.

A model of how the palace may have looked

A view of the ruins of Knossos, as they appear today (right)

A male Minoan bull leaper is flanked by two female helpers on one of the many frescoes in the palace.

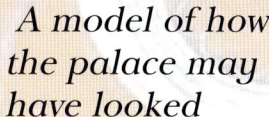

A Minoan golden bee

Minoan Culture

The Minoans were great seafarers and traded with many other countries. They sold goods such as grain, wine, oil, and saffron in return for precious metals and other luxury items.

Minoan pots have been found all over the eastern Mediterranean.

THE DEATH OF PETE MARSH

"O, great Beltane, we offer this sacrifice…"

As these words rang out across the marsh, the man kneeling on the ground let out a low moan. But it was useless to put up a struggle. His fate was sealed.

He was a man in his mid-twenties, of high status. He was possibly a Druid—certainly his hands showed no signs of hard labor. Apart from a fox-fur armband, he was naked.

Many times before, he had offered sacrifices to the gods. Soon it would be his turn to be the sacrifice. For years, the Romans had persecuted the Druids. Now, on the great feast of Beltane, the gods' help was to be called on. And for that, the man would have to die.

His end, when it came, was violent. First, he was strangled; then he was hit on the head with the blunt end of an axe. Finally, his throat was cut. Then his body was thrown face down in the marsh and left to rot…

FIND OUT MORE

RITUAL MURDER

In 1984, a local peat-cutter found parts of the man's body at Lindow Moss in Cheshire, England. Four years later, more of the body was discovered. The man was named "Pete Marsh," or "Lindow Man." Scientific tests showed that he had died around 2,000 years ago.

Remains preserved in Pete Marsh's stomach show that his last meal consisted of simple grain bread and mistletoe pollen (above).

OVERKILL

Like Lindow Man, many other bog bodies show evidence of violent deaths. It would seem that they, too, were killed as human sacrifices to the Celtic gods. The three forms of deadly violence suffered by Lindow Man may have appealed to three different gods.

Lindow Moss, where Pete Marsh was found, is a raised peat bog—one of a number of unique habitats where bog bodies are found.

Huldremose Woman, found in Denmark, is 2,000 years old. She had her right arm hacked off and was stabbed repeatedly in the legs and feet. Was she too a victim of ritual murder?

MORE BOG BODIES

Northern Europe's peat bogs have offered other ancient victims. The combination of acidic water, cold temperature, and lack of oxygen has preserved skin and internal organs. Their bones may be dissolved, but the evidence of how they perished remains indelible.

Tollund Man (above) was found in a peat bog in Denmark. A leather strap around his neck showed that he had been strangled or hanged.

Grauballe Man (below) is one of the best preserved bog bodies in the world. Found in Jutland, in Denmark, his body dates from around 290 BCE.

Grauballe Man's preserved hand still has its fingerprints (above).

Yde Girl (below), from the Netherlands, was found with a belt wrapped around her neck. Sixteen years old, she died sometime in the first century CE and has been reconstructed (right).

The skeleton, skin, hair, stomach, and brain of Bocksten Man (below right) are very well preserved. A medieval Swedish murder victim, Bockstein Man was thrown into a lake, which later became a bog.

BURIAL AT SUTTON HOO
"Farewell, brave soul, may your journey be swift..."

Holding his burning torch high, the warrior uttered the words. As he spoke, he gazed down at the boat and the body lying inside. Then he gave the order for the boat and its occupant to be buried.

Days before, the magnificent oak ship had been hauled up the steep slope from the Deben River to the brow of the hill at Sutton Hoo, near Woodbridge, Suffolk, in the eastern UK. It was lowered into a deep trench, its prow facing toward the east.

The ship was over 88 feet (27 meters) long. In its center, they had constructed a burial chamber with timber walls and a pitched roof. With great care and solemn ceremony, the body of the man was placed inside. Around him, his warriors then laid out the weapons, symbolic objects, and treasures that he would need for his journey to the afterlife.

After a final show of respect, the ship was covered over by a great mound of earth. Rising high above the horizon, the mound stood as a fitting memorial to a brave and powerful leader and created a visual symbol of strength for those who used the nearby waterway. This magnificent funeral was to be the last of its kind at Sutton Hoo…

FIND OUT MORE

WHOSE GRAVE?

Some 1,300 years later, in 1939, archaeologists began work on the largest of 16 ancient burial mounds at Sutton Hoo. Beneath it, they discovered the ship grave but still did not know who had been buried there.

DEATH OF A KING?

Judging by the magnificent objects found inside the grave, it belonged to a man of great wealth and status. This may have been Raedwald, a powerful Anglo-Saxon ruler of East Anglia who died in about 625 CE.

A picture of the Sutton Hoo dig in progress in 1939

One of two shoulder clasps made of gold inlaid with garnets

The most famous finds were the fragments of an ornate warrior's helmet.

Some of the emptied burial mounds at Sutton Hoo have been reconstructed to resemble their ancient state.

The metalworking on this golden shield decoration is exquisite.

A reconstruction of how the entire shield may have looked (far left)

A replica showing the helmet in all its glory

TREASURE TROVE

An extraordinary number of beautiful and costly grave goods were found in the burial chamber. They included gold and garnet jewelry, silver bowls and cups, a lyre, weapons, and fragments of fine clothes. They have allowed experts to put together a detailed picture of Anglo-Saxon life in the first century CE.

How the owner of the grave items might have looked.

Golden coins were also in the hoard.

A magnificent gold buckle (below), decorated with Saxon symbols

Replica of the lyre

THE LOST CITY OF COPÁN

"Look—an ancient temple, lost to the ages!"

As he spoke, John Lloyd Stephens stared in wonder at the sight in front of him. Through the tangles of branches and jungle vines stood an ancient stone temple. Had he reached his goal at last?

An American diplomat and explorer, Stephens had read many earlier accounts of mysterious lost cities dotted around Central America. Greatly intrigued, he and his companion, Frederick Catherwood, set off for Honduras to investigate.

For weeks, the two men explored the jungle with the help of local guides, but no one knew where the ruins lay. Then, in November 1859, they made a breakthrough. Among the dense undergrowth, they could see the tumbled remains of old stone buildings. Astonishingly, they had stumbled on Copán, an ancient Mayan city, lost for over a thousand years.

Stephens and Catherwood spent several weeks clearing the site and making drawings. Among the ruins were large stones known as stelae, covered in hieroglyphics, or picture writing. Frustratingly, they could not read what was written. If the hieroglyphics could be deciphered, what secrets would they be able to tell?

FIND OUT MORE

CLUES TO THE PAST

The hieroglyphics on the stelae were later deciphered and found to give the main dates and events during a king's rule. They help to show that, from the 5th to 9th centuries CE, Copán had been one of the greatest and most prosperous of Mayan cities.

A painting of a stela by Catherwood, showing one of the city's kings

Ruins of Copán

Apart from the stelae, Stephens and Catherwood discovered the ruins of ancient pyramid-temples, plazas, and palaces. There was also a large court for playing a Mayan ballgame. Many of these buildings have now been restored by archaeologists.

A hieroglyphic staircase of 63 steps rises to a height of 80 feet (24 m) – the longest text carved into stone by the Maya.

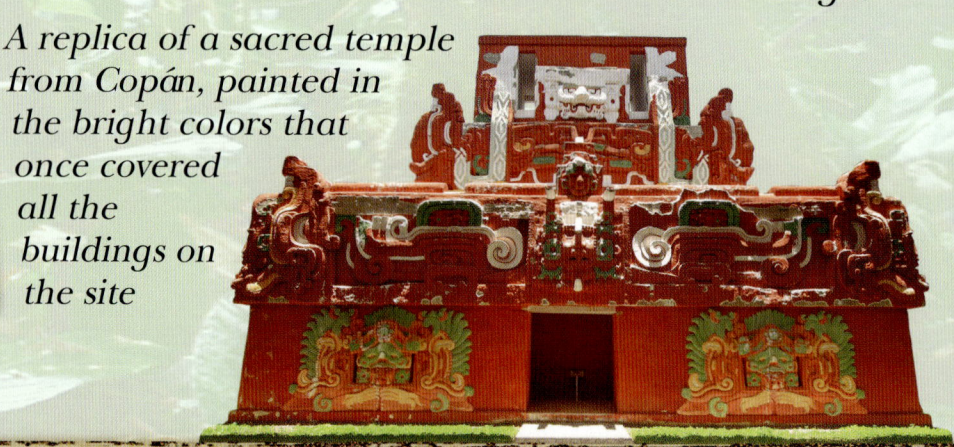

A replica of a sacred temple from Copán, painted in the bright colors that once covered all the buildings on the site

The ancient ball court at Copán

CRACKING THE CODE

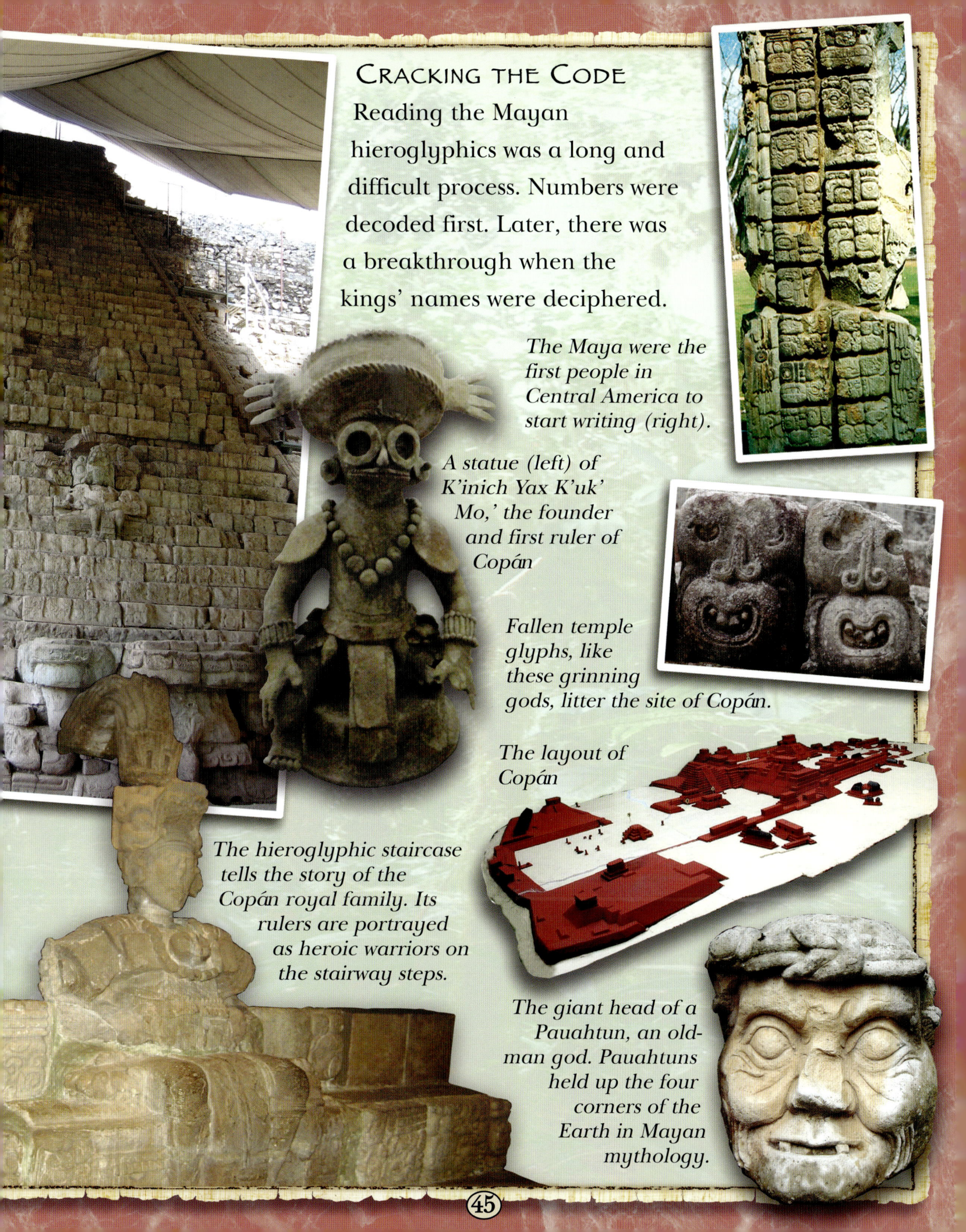

Reading the Mayan hieroglyphics was a long and difficult process. Numbers were decoded first. Later, there was a breakthrough when the kings' names were deciphered.

The Maya were the first people in Central America to start writing (right).

A statue (left) of K'inich Yax K'uk' Mo,' the founder and first ruler of Copán

Fallen temple glyphs, like these grinning gods, litter the site of Copán.

The layout of Copán

The hieroglyphic staircase tells the story of the Copán royal family. Its rulers are portrayed as heroic warriors on the stairway steps.

The giant head of a Pauahtun, an old-man god. Pauahtuns held up the four corners of the Earth in Mayan mythology.

GLOSSARY

Archaeologist A person who studies the past by looking at ancient places and objects.

Artifacts Human-made objects of archaeological interest from the past.

Antechamber A smaller room used as an entryway to a larger, main room.

Canopic jar An urn used in ancient Egypt to store the internal organs from bodies that were mummified.

Druids A priestly group in ancient Celtic culture.

Embalmers In ancient Egypt, people who prepared dead bodies for mummification.

Hieroglyphs Pictures or signs used in several ancient systems of writing, representing objects, ideas, or sounds.

Indelible Something that cannot be easily removed or washed away.

Labyrinth A maze-like structure.

Mummies Dead bodies that were washed, embalmed, and wrapped in bandages to preserve them for the afterlife.

Paleontologist A person who studies fossils and the prehistoric past.

Pumice A type of volcanic rock that is lighter than water.

Sarcophagus A stone coffin that usually has decorations or engravings.

Scarab An ancient Egyptian gem or stone cut in the form of a beetle.

Skirmish A minor battle in a larger war.

Stelae Large stone slabs, engraved with extracts of ancient texts.

FURTHER INFORMATION

ORGANIZATIONS AND WEB SITES

The Smithsonian Institute
1000 Jefferson Drive, SW
Washington, D.C
(202) 633 - 1000
email: info@si.edu
Web site: http://www.si.edu

British Museum
Great Russell Street
London WC1B 3DG
United Kingdom
Tel.: +44 (0)20 7323 8838
Web site:
http://www.britishmuseum.org

The Sutton Hoo Society
32 Mariners Way
Aldeburgh
Suffolk IP15 5QH
United Kingdom
email: info@suttonhoo.org
Web site: http://www.suttonhoo.org

Copan Ruins and Museum
Copan, Honduras
email: questions@thisishonduras.com
Web site:
http://thisishonduras.com/Copan_Ruinas.htm.

FOR FURTHER READING

Capek, Michael. *Emperor Qin's Terra Cotta Army (Unearthing Ancient Worlds)*. Minneapolis, MN: Twenty-First Century Books, 2008.

Fontes, Justine, Ron Fontes, and Gordon Purcell. *The Trojan Horse: The Fall of Troy: A Greek Legend*. Minneapolis, MN: Lerner Publishing Group, 2007.

Ganeri, Anita, and David West. *Lost in the Bermuda Triangle and Other Mysteries.* New York, NY: Rosen Publishing, 2012.

Shone, Rob, and Nick Spender. *Graphic Discoveries: Ancient Treasures.* New York, NY: Rosen Publishing, 2009.

INDEX

A
archaeologist, 11, 16, 17, 25, 32, 40, 44,

B
Brain, "Bob," 27, 28
Broom, Robert, 27

C
Carnarvon, Lord, 7
Carter, Howard, 7, 8
Catherwood, Frederick, 43, 44
Copán, Honduras, 42, 43, 44, 45

D
De Alcubierre, Joachim, 24

E
Egypt, 4, 8
Evans, Arthur, 32

G
Great Pyramid, the, 9

H
Helen, 14, 17
Herculaneum, 23
Homer, 15, 16, 17
Honduras, 42

K
Knossos, Crete, 30–33

L
Labyrinth, 32, 33

M
"Marsh, Pete," 34–35
Mayan, 43–45
Menelaus, 8
Minoan civilization, 30–33

O
Ötzi (ice man), 19–21

P
Pompeii, 22–25

Q
Qin Shi Huangdi, 11–13

R
Ramesses II, 9
Roman, 17, 24, 35

S
Santorini, 31
Schliemann, Heinrich, 16–17
Simon, Erika, 18–19
Stephens, John Lloyd, 42–44
Sterkfontein caves, 28
Sutton Hoo, 38–40
Swartkrans caves, 26–29

T
Terracotta Army, 10–13
Troy, 14–17
Tutankhamun, 6–9

V
Valley of the Kings, 9
Vesuvius, Mount, 22–23

X
Xiyang Village, 11

WEB SITES

Due to the changing nature of Internet links, Rosen Publishing has developed an online list of Web sites related to the subject of this book. This site is updated regularly. Please use this link to access this list: http://www.rosenlinks.com/ita/tut